New Ground

New Ground

A painting and fishing holiday in Wester Ross

By R.H. Eadie

To Bob

With Best Wishes

Jean Eadie

Edited and designed by Jean M. Eadie

ISBN-0-9533343-0-9

Printed by BPC-AUP Aberdeen Ltd.
for the Publisher: Mrs Jean M. Eadie
22 Leggart Terrace, Aberdeen, AB12 5TX

Colour reproduction by Icon Reprographics(Aberdeen).

Cover Picture:- The tidal pool, Inverasdale, Wester Ross-shire

FOREWORD

My husband loved outdoor life - walking, cycling, camping, painting, fishing. He also liked to write, and sometimes after a particularly enjoyable holiday he would write it all down whilst it was still fresh in his mind.

Occasionally he would decide to make it into a small journal and add some delightful illustrations from sketches he had done on holiday.

He and I shared the same interests, so I decided to put together this book from the first holiday he wrote about after we were married and I have added paintings and sketches by both of us.

We found Inverasdale on Loch Ewe, Wester Ross, in 1964 and loved the natural unspoilt beauty of the district so much that we came back for the next 25 years. Painting in all kinds of weather - from the car when we had to; seeing the same places from different angles and in different lights, each time ending up with a new picture. Fishing many of the hill lochs of which there were dozens - with unpronounceable Gaelic names - and watching the bird life, seeing birds that were never in any British bird book - probably migrants stopping for a few days of rest before moving on to another country; picking up beautiful sea shells and finding unusual wild flowers.....

This book is about our first holiday, and if you like it there could be others.....

Rowland Hill Eadie
1905 – 1991

NEW GROUND

As long as the road slides round a bend

We've got to see where it goes.

It's a human fault – a curious trend

And it leads us – goodness knows.

To many things we might never have seen,

To many a glorious view,

But the joy of discovery keeps us keen

To go on again – and we do!

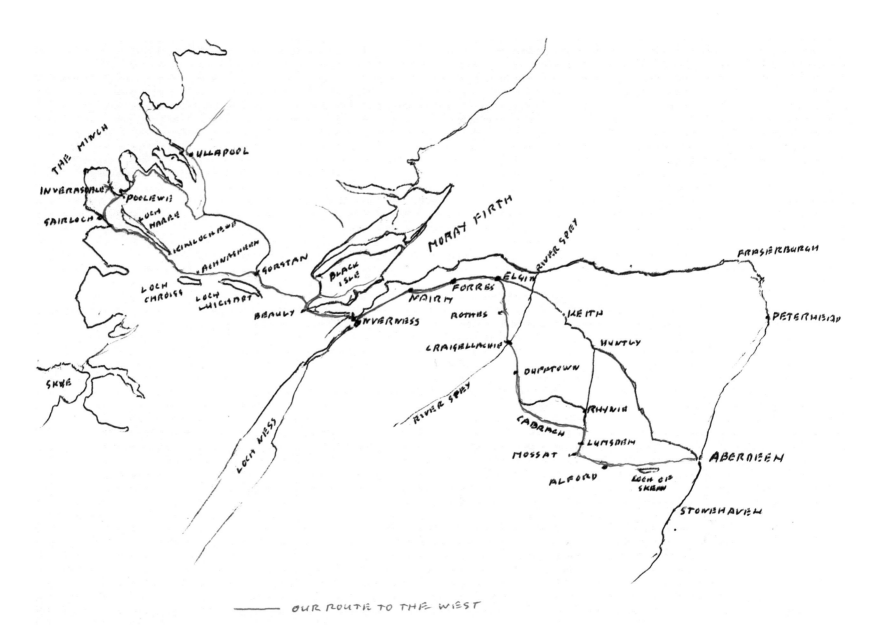

VIII

Chapter I

Cuckoo! Cuckoo! Cuckoo!

"Who does that bird think is cuckoo? –and where is he anyway?" There wasn't a single tree in sight up where the sound came from - just a broken jumble of rocks and heathery tufts backing steeply from the narrow road to the piled grey cliffs, and we couldn't see a single movement.

"Cuckoo! Cuckoo! Cuckoo! Cuckoo! Cuckoo! Tut, tut, tut, tut!" Still no sign of him though we gazed long and hard at what seemed to be the exact spot of origin. And of course when we turned away he moved like a ghost and mocked us from a different quarter. Then, further over, a collared dove called "Coo-COOO-coo, Coo-COOO-coo" over and over, just as persistent as the cuckoo; while out on the water the eerie sound of the Great Northern Diver was heard occasionally, with its long wailing cry and weird sort of laughing sound, that makes the back of

CUCKOO

COLLARED DOVE

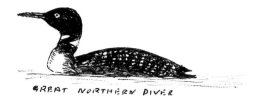

GREAT NORTHERN DIVER

your neck creep if you don't know what it is. That's just three of the many different birds to be seen and heard over on the West Coast. All that came later, of course, so let's start at the beginning of the holiday.....

It was June 1964 and the year of the Typhoid outbreak in Aberdeen, and we had slipped quietly out of town and headed North with perhaps slightly guilty feelings in view of the medical situation, but we went with our doctor's permission and blessing. We had no idea where we were going, just North and West and ...? Wherever the car took us!

We left Aberdeen on a glorious Saturday morning with a sense of adventure. Out by Alford and up to Lumsden and off over the Cabrach to Dufftown. Then on to the Moray Firth and along to Inverness. Even with thin rain showers now, drifting lazily over the wooded higher ground of the Black Isle, we had a curious feeling of 'going home' as we circled the end of the Beauly Firth and headed round the shore by Redcastle. We had been to the Black Isle for varying spells so often before, in many different types of weather, that the

place had come to look attractive at any time. Our snug camp site was vacant and the tent was soon up, though the usual keen enjoyment of this first night was a trifle marred by the need to perform the operation in a steady drizzle of fine rain.

The old, open cooking fireplace spot was still there, partly smothered in grass and sporting a magnificent growth of spiky thistle from the ash-bed of our previous fires. All this greenery, rather regretfully, had to be sacrificed in the interest of week-end hot meals, but it didn't take long to get everything tidy and some very welcome food prepared. The rain had cleared by then and it had turned chilly, so a short brisk walk was the obvious solution to restore full circulation before we turned in to the comfort of cosy sleeping bags.

Sunday morning was bright and clear and the air soon became almost oppressively hot as we lazed in our very sheltered little circle of bushes by the edge of the firth. It was a restful day of recovery before we crossed to the West Coast the following day, and we relished the opportunity to sit in quiet comfort listening to the distant sound of rushing traffic dashing north and south along the road to Beauly and Inverness on the far shore.

During the afternoon, clouds drifted over the big hills of Strath Glass, and long before evening we knew we were in for a thunderstorm. The wind which usually precedes such an atmospheric disturbance, ruffled the long sheet of water in sudden, darting, dark patches, and the sky became more and more overcast until it assumed the yellow, purple bruised-blue look that promised a sudden eruption of violence.

Eventually it came – after we had felt the hair on the back of our necks prickling for some time – a ripping, crackling, zig-zag of lightning that split the 'hanging' atmosphere, and sent the following thunder crashing and echoing overhead and round the top of the long waterway in a riot of sound.

We were not unduly worried, for we had been through bad thunderstorms and gales on many former nights with the same trusty tent, and we had time to make everything snug before settling to a meal. The hard hiss of torrential rain lashing the water several feet away could be clearly heard, and although we were still unaffected, the other shore had disappeared behind a grey curtain, and a dark moving line showed where the edge of the deluge advanced towards us with steady persistence.

When the first drops hit the tent they sounded like bullets, and within a few seconds we could hardly hear ourselves speak through the rattle of raindrops on drum-tight canvas. The wind came with the downpour and the tent was lashed and buffeted unmercifully, while shattering thunder ripped the sky to shreds, and every few minutes another searing flash flickered over the streaming tent walls.

We ate in comfort, glad of our good fortune in being on a fixed site instead of looking for a camping corner when the storm came, and watching the worst of the thundery rain wash across Inverness and drift away over the distant hills towards Speyside.

"It's past – we're lucky to have missed the worst of it", we said to each other, but by heck we were wrong! We were in bed later on when the storm circled and came back over us on its way north, catching the tent on the more open unsheltered side next to the firth with the usual full accompaniment of flash-bangs, wildly vicious bursts of wind and rain,

'Thunderstorm over the Black Isle'.

and seemingly determined, but luckily unsuccessful, efforts to sweep our little outfit off the ground.

Ultimately the storm tailed off to a faint soft whisper of rain; the wind passed and left a curiously empty washed out sort of silence – and we slept.

Chapter II

Monday morning was again fine, and though a light shower drifted over just after breakfast had been cooked, the sun and the breeze soon had the canvas dry and we packed the tent in good condition.

Muir of Ord was our first port of call, to hunt out milk and certain favoured supplies we had sampled on earlier visits, but the shop of our quest was unexpectedly shut and we had to look elsewhere.

Our road to the West lay ahead, by Contin of the flower patched hedges to Garve and Achnasheen, and eventually we stopped for a meal high on the moor beyond Loch Chroisg, where the view was superbly panoramic and delightfully colourful. The hillside across the valley invited inspection and very soon the powerful binoculars picked out four deer feeding slowly over a grassy shelf high up in one of the stream hollows. One of the beasts was a big fellow with a splendid-looking set of antlers in velvet. The other three seemed to be hinds, and the position they were in gave them the greatest possible measure of safety on the open hillside, with views ranging wide for miles on either side. A single beast feeding alone further up also carried velvet antlers and had the rich red-brown coat indicating a younger animal, but otherwise the only apparent life on the hillsides was provided by a few scattered white dots where sheep fed.

At the near end of the loch, the glasses showed a stone sheep fank (fold) on a grassy shelf by the water, and what seemed to be the remains of a small stone bothy or cottage with a vague indication of a grass track going away from it. Probably, like so many other highland glens, this ground at one time held a group of small crofters' homes and the old track was doubtless one of the bridle paths and cattle routes used long before the present road was made. It must have been a really rough undertaking to wring a living from that wild countryside.

The long steep drop of Glen Docherty to the top of Loch Maree soon opened ahead, and before long we were down on the lochside road dodging through trees and round tricky rock outcrops along that lovely stretch of water. Over on the north side,

*Across Loch Maree towards Slioch. That
curious mountain on top of a mountain.*

towering above the steeply climbing moors, Slioch stood aloof and dignified, brooding no doubt over the bustling tourist traffic that flashed past in such shocking contrast to the easier and more leisurely movement of kilted Highlanders and horses and cattle this district had favoured in former dreamy days.

The hotel, hidden amongst massed rhododendrons, had the usual complement of big cars, boats and fishing rods. Then we were suddenly amongst fir plantations which stream away to the skyline from Slattadale. Beyond these we went to cross the moor by the hill lochs to Kerrysdale with its partially lost glory. Below the road in that steep glen, where the falls in the gorge under the roadside retaining wall used to be a regular tourist attraction, the river bed was a jumbled mass of dry boulders with scarcely a gleam of water anywhere. The big pipeline now keeps the road company in steep swoops to the powerhouse, where the scene changes again, and amongst the rugged old Scots firs the river has once more that tumbling, bustling flow so attractive in such a setting.

Alas, no fishing is allowed – officially – and practically every little green patch by the roadside holds a notice of warning that 'no camping' is permitted. Just in case! but *all* the fish that go up from the tide's edge don't survive, and the local people know where, and how, to get a salmon when they want one!

We were told later about the tragedy which had happened in that same glen under such circumstances. A salmon was required for some unexpected guests, and an old man and his wife went off to a chosen spot with a net – on a Sunday! The water was high and it seems that the old chap became tangled in his own net and was pulled into the river, where he was drowned in full view of his wife. The fatality was regarded as a judgement – not for poaching, but for going after a salmon – *on the Sabbath!*

On the level ground beyond the woods, we turned off on to the Badachro/Port Henderson road. It was well-surfaced and went gliding and swooping through tangled oak and birch woods to come back suddenly to the side of the Gair Loch at Shieldaig, on the edge of a very sheltered

The river Kerry – Kerrysdale

picturesque little anchorage which seemed to glow with rich colour. Brightly painted small boats swung at anchor on deep green warm-looking water, which ringed a tree grown island edged with a line of red and green rocks. Outside these, on the edge of the tide-line, lay a beautifully contrasting mat of yellow and orange seaweed, shading in places to that elusive green-brown which appears only in tangled sea growth.

The island held only one house, leaning against the clean sloping turf amongst a straggle of trees, and across the narrow channel to the mainland lay other two cottages – one with an outstanding bright red roof – snuggling into the hillside and protected by hazel and birch clumps. Out beyond, where the passage opened to the main sea loch, a stretch of sun-dappled water was backed in the distance by white cottage dots on the misty blue hillside of the far shore. But we wanted camping space and had so far seen no suitable corner, so we had to go on after promising ourselves a sketching return – from somewhere.

Earlier that day, as we came through the big woods by the shores of Loch Maree, a roe deer had suddenly broken from the cover of the trees and skipped daintily across the road not twenty five yards in front of us, and now, as we rounded a corner among the birches on the Badachro road, another one, darker and older, did exactly the same. In each case ours was the only car on the spot at the time although these narrow roads carried a fairly steady stream of vehicles. We marvelled at the strange chance that we, who saw roe and red deer often on our own countryside, should have these glimpses of wild life which would have thrilled other holiday makers less fortunate than ourselves; though part of Loch Maree ground is a National Park area, and the Forestry Commission employees have no great love for them as they destroy young trees.

However, we pressed on in our voyage of exploration.

A few cottages, a hotel and a small shop-cum Post Office, then an attractive loch, followed by another colourful bay containing one or two white yachts at anchor and the pathetic, bare ribs of a handful of former wooden fishing vessels. Still another 'fishy' looking loch, a long bare moor stretch with nothing but sky behind - which suggested open sea – and finally a steep dipping road twisting through sweeps of lovely red sand to Erradale. As we sped along we mentally marked a number of those places for later exploration with the paint box, and since no attractive camping ground appeared to be available in that area, we eventually turned in our tracks, rejoined the Kerrysdale road in due course, and went on through the magnificently colourful, towering old Scots firs and banks of still flowering rhododendrons by the riverside, to come down past the holiday caravans to Gairloch at the entrance to Flowerdale.

By then, however, we were out again on the windy side of the sea loch and knew we would probably have to go on over the next hill to the sheltered coast at Poolewe. This we eventually did, and turning into the narrow road past Poolewe on the south side of Loch Ewe, we stopped at a lay-by to look out the loch to see if any place looked suitable for camping. It was a bit dull and looked like rain and we were getting anxious about finding a place, especially as the sides of the road

seemed to be covered with bracken - which would not be very comfortable when the midges 'came out to play'! Just then the sun suddenly shone on one particular spot away down the lochside. A patch of green grass – mm! that looks hopeful, and off we went. It was – we had arrived at Inverasdale, and a small sheep fank promised a level dry place for the tent. All we needed was permission, and on asking at a house nearby we were told it was common ground so no one would mind.

We soon had the tent up on lovely short firm turf, with the car alongside as a windbreak. Within an hour a trail of wood smoke drifted away from the bank behind the tent – we were HOME. This was our base for the next fortnight.

The wind was still with us and though we were very well sheltered for the time being on the lochside shelf below the high bank where the road was, we suspected that a swing of a point or two in the direction of the breeze might easily land us in trouble. It did change from time to time during our stay, and we kept moving the car from one side of the tent to the other to ease the buffeting, but even

'Through Poolewe to Loch Ewe'.

Camp at
Inverasdale

so, we did not keep entirely free of trouble. About three a.m. one morning, in spite of boulder stabilisers behind every tent peg and all round the hessian underflaps, I was wakened by Jean's query – "Ron, what do we do about this?". "This" – was a lovely big balloon of green canvas spreading itself over her camp bed. The wind was literally hammering the tent, but luckily it was dry outside, so out I went with the mallet to refix two of the side guy ropes from which the pegs had been uprooted. With these fixed and everything checked, I dived back into the tent and the comfort of my warm

sleeping bag and had scarcely got my head on the pillow when the rain hit the canvas in a tearing squall. One ear on the pillow and the other under the thickness of the sleeping bag made a glorious difference to the sound, and we went back to sleep.

By the time we cleared up that first meal, however, the mocking cuckoo was calling from somewhere away above and behind the road, long and repeatedly, and we were at the stage of saying – "Oh! cuckoo yourself"! Even a short time later when we went up to the road to walk along the line of houses towards the skyline, we could not catch a glimpse of the persistent songster, and in fact during the whole of our two week stay not once did we see that elusive grey ghost bird though he was constantly with us.

That first evening stroll towards the north-west showed us several little corners that looked worthy of further examination in different light, and it was quite late before we turned back from the high ground away beyond the school, near which we caught a glimpse of a big intriguing looking loch lying in a dip of the moor. Obviously there was much to see at closer quarters.

Over the next day or two we explored as much as we could between showers, and Jean made friendly contacts with one or two of the cottagers, who were extremely helpful regarding vans and sources of supplies. Firewood was a problem at first as there were only a few stunted grey willows near at hand, but we had passed a thicket of trees along the road from Poolewe, so by taking the car along there and loading up with dead wood, we had ample for our fire. That little wood consisted of hazel, birch and oak trees clothing the steep roadside bank, but below the road the ground was soft and marshy with a profusion of gigantic foxgloves of various shades. In addition to the usual dark reddish purple, there were fine specimens of white, with sprinklings of a lovely lavender type which I had not seen before. These ranged from a very pale to a deep shade and practically every one carried a first class head on a strongly conical plant.

That first Monday night was reasonably dry and peaceful but by morning the weather had deteriorated. There was a strong wind, and whilst it was blowing from behind the hills above the road, it was playing strange tricks on the loch close to the beach. The turbulent air currents were upset by the vacuum caused by the cliff face, and whilst they mainly missed the tent on its snug level edge, they plummeted down on to the loch and literally exploded, running themselves to pieces in squally cat-paws which spread out in all directions.

FOXGLOVE.
IN ALL SHADES FROM WHITE TO DEEP PINK

Chapter III

On Tuesday morning my first job was to complete the fireplace, so that we could have our traditional camping breakfast of bacon, sausage, egg and tomato, with a soft roll and oatcakes and marmalade, and a "billy" of tea. That really put a good lining on our stomachs and meant that if we went out sketching for the day, an apple and a biscuit at lunchtime would keep us going till we came back to camp for an evening meal.

We brought one or two bits and pieces with us for the fireplace, namely three sticks cut to a suitable size for the uprights and one to lie across the top, just in case no suitable wood was available. From this a strong piece of telephone wire was suspended, bent to shape, to hang the old black kettle on for tea. This kettle had seen a lot of use and was well coated with wood smoke and ideal for our purpose. I had also picked up a very useful piece of equipment – an old iron grid with legs on which sat the frying pan and it had made lots of camping breakfasts. Several large stones

THE CAMP FIRE
AT INVERBDALE

from the beach in front of us made the fireplace, and as this was a sheep fank there were odd pieces of corrugated iron lying about, so a small piece at either side of the fireplace made ideal wind breaks. Then one unusual curved stone made a comfy seat, – that was it complete, we were all set. "Breakfast coming up".

We had just finished our meal and done the washing up, when the hills at the end of the loch behind Poolewe disappeared and rain came sweeping down the loch. We made ourselves quite snug in the tent, and for most of the day sat happily and comfortably writing and painting, while passing motorists doubtless pitied the "poor campers" and guessed we must be pretty miserable. Our tent was a cottage one and we could stand upright quite easily. Two naval canvas camp beds and down filled sleeping bags kept us off the ground and warm and dry at night. We also had two collapsible canvas chairs and travelling rugs and were wearing warm kilts. All of which kept us warm in bad weather – and you get quite a bit of that on the west coast! We even had wellingtons and macs, but we found the local people didn't bother with raincoats unless it was lashing down, and just carried on regardless.

They were a naturally friendly, completely incurious group of people who thought that curiosity was not polite. Even the children did not come near when we stopped to sketch by the roadside as town children always do, though everyone was always ready to help or to give information at any time.

In the afternoon it cleared to more occasional showers and we went out to do some quick pen sketches, and in one longer dry spell I went along the road towards Poolewe and climbed up the side of one of the clear little burns which dropped through a dip in the hills and looked as if it might be the outflow of a small loch. As I climbed I struck a rough and very steep track which went up in a series of curves and swoops to squeeze through the gap below the little cliff where the burn tumbled into view. Here and there on the stony earth there appeared to be faint wheel tracks, but I could scarcely imagine any sort of vehicle on a hillside path of that sort. I was, therefore, more than a little surprised to see a broken caterpillar tractor wheel lying on the scree below the cliff, and just beyond that a well made heavy wood bridge over the stream. A trifle more exploration explained the mystery. The top waters of a stream had been tapped and channelled into a reservoir tank, and the recently dug track of the outgoing pipeline showed where the fresh water had been led down to the cottages below. I could see no loch at the top of the little glen, however, so I set off back to camp, wondering not a little at the task undertaken by the men who had carved that track out of the hillside and transported the necessary materials up to the heights of the bridge, and the building of the reservoir.

That part of the North-west was one of the Government crofting rehabilitation areas, where crofts that had been practically or wholly derelict had been opened up again and re-settled, with grants for land improvement and cropping, electric power and water laid on, roads re-surfaced, and every encouragement given towards establishing a

lively productive community. Almost all the cottages had "Bed and Breakfast" or "Accommodation" signs. The men do a bit of line or lobster creel fishing, and occasionally get Council or Government contract work on the roads or special schemes, and they appear to be making a satisfactory go of it, though a Skye man to whom I spoke of this type of scheme seemed to be rather in doubt about the ultimate result.

Everywhere we could see evidence of the old "lazy bed system" which the crofters used to operate in earlier days. Slopes above the shore still

showed this ridged form of cultivation beds, though the heather and moor grass had overgrown the spots many years ago. The old system they employed was to turn over the thin top soil of a strip wherever this was possible, cover it with a thick layer if seaweed from the shore, then dig a ditch along each side of the bed and spread over the dug earth and any more they could transport to the spot by creel or wheelbarrow, to form a raised broad bank of turfy soil on a sort of hot-bed of kelp. After this had been allowed to weather down and rot for some time, holes were made in the surface, and a potato dropped into each so that in due course, a crop of potatoes could be taken from each little area. Generally a series of these beds existed side by side, and the whole lot gave the slopes a corrugated appearance which they have retained, and which is still easily seen near the old ruins.

After tea, as so often happened during that first week, the evening proved to be by far the best part of the day, so when the tide had gone back to its full limit we followed it out through the seaweed and small rock pools to the shingle beds at the mouth of the little burn, and looked around for shells. We found nothing more than the common ones which lie around in thousands on most shores. There were limpets, blue mussels, cockles and whelks and a sprinkling of trough shells and some broken pieces of large spindle, but the shore was far too full of small loose rocks for any delicate shells to survive – or so we thought at the time – for nothing attractive caught our eyes.

The gulls apparently thought otherwise, for when we went back to the tent they came back to the seaweed covered rocks in front of us and became extremely busy. We sat watching them through binoculars to see what they were looking for, and it was soon obvious that they were crab hunting. One would strut along slowly, looking here and there until suddenly it would shoot out its bill, grab a long trail of seaweed and deftly and quickly flick it over to see what moved underneath.

Sometimes it was apparently a small crab that failed to find shelter, and it was quickly seized and swallowed without ceremony.

These gulls did not welcome the presence of the

old craggy heron, and would rise screaming and scolding and circling, if he glided down to his favourite rock near them. Quite close along the shore a long narrow, sloping stone pier went out to deep water, with a marking pole topped by a large bleached ball showing where the end of the stonework dropped off into deeper water. At the inland end of this tiny landing slip, where a steep little roadway came down from the main shore road, the concrete base shape of a small military hut was still quite easily recognised and we wondered how often that quiet shore had seen much more sinister comings and goings from much less obvious camps than ours, in former wartime days.

Wednesday morning was dry but dull and misty on the hills away behind Poolewe and the breakfast fire gave little difficulty, even though fuel was at that time almost a minus quantity. By the time we had stocked up with our usual meal, the cloud had lifted and the sun had changed the whole view. Intriguing cloud shadows chased each other over the contours of the piled up hills, and since the obvious thing to do was to go sketching,

mid afternoon saw us going back to Poolewe and crossing the hill road south over to Gairloch.

Loch Maree looked a perfect picture from the very well known touring bus viewpoint above Tollie croft, but we passed on towards Gairloch and the corners that had captivated us during our first exploratory glimpses when we were camp-site hunting. Over on that side there was a fair breeze and the white wave caps shone brilliantly against the peacock blue of the sand fringed bay.

We sat for a few minutes on a grassy roadside view point high above the water looking down and over that magnificent stretch of sea and landscape. Endless peaks piling up behind each other across the bay, seemed to carry every possible variation of shape and shade, while off towards the west we could see the rather hazy outline of the north-east corner of Skye in the distance beyond the Port Henderson point. Years ago I had sat at the other end of that view, high on the shelves of the Quirang above Staffin Bay on Skye, painting the view across the strait to the Ross-shire hills – the present position in reverse. But all that colour simply fostered our urge to paint, and we slid

STRATH, GAIRLOCH

down to the loch side.

At the foot of the hill the cottages and orange rocks of sun-steeped Strath proved too strong an attraction from an artistic point of view, and we turned off onto that so far unexplored shore road and dawdled along from one stopping place to the next, looking, and admiring, and dashing off quick sketches here and there as we went. Eventually we slipped into a small open parking place in Strath close to the post office, and while Jean went shopping for one or two necessities in the food line, I sat down to do a quick painting.

Just below the open space, a little stream bustled under a small white bridge and wound down through the boulders into the salt water, and out beyond the burn mouth, past one or two ruinous old red sandstone walls, the sun-flecked water was backed by a rising jumble of wooded slopes and heathery mounds, fading back into the distant peaks of the National Park grounds, from the top of Glen Torridon to Beinn Alligan. Later investigation of the Strath area on the map showed that the Strath burn comes down from five good-sized lochs away back in the hills, and since that area

STRATH, GAIRLOCH

'Flowerdale'
(This stream joined the sea at Gairloch).

'Gairloch Pier'

also holds a great number of smaller lochans, we promised ourselves some more exploration at a later date.

The need of that moment, however, was something to eat, so we circled back along the main road to the sheltered end of the loch at Flowerdale and turned around towards the pier, where we toasted in brilliant sun while we had our snack. There again all sorts of corners offered sketching subjects and we lingered to soak up colourful details for sketching another day before going on up the Kerrysdale road through the long stretch of glorious old Scotch fir trees.

A short time later we were again down by the waters edge among the big oak trees and birches on the Shieldaig road, but the tide was out and the formerly attractive corners proved rather a disappointment. Big stretches of bare rock and seaweed took the place of the luminous green water we had seen on our first visit, and in any event we found that suitable parking places just did not exist at the right places for the views we fancied. So again we dashed off quick pen sketches and notes and went on to the hill lochs further out.

We watched fishermen on boats casting and drifting on the lochs, then turned back to do a painting of a long narrow stretch of water which bordered the road and had a splendid open view beyond the keeper's cottage overlooking the loch and the valley down to the bay. That done, we felt it was a shame to waste the remaining sunshine, so went back to the Kerrysdale road and turned up the glen towards the power house at the foot of the gorge.

Just over the Kerry bridge a small pale blue lorry laden with scrap metal was parked by the roadside, and a family of travelling road folk had camped in an old brown bell tent on a level bit of the moor. They had a good fire going, and we felt pretty certain they'd need it later on because they were in a glory hole for midges! Two kiddies waved us a friendly greeting as we passed, and we waved back little thinking we'd be seeing that same hawker family in various corners of the district for the next two weeks.

Further up the glen we each did another painting where masses of glorious flowering rhododendrons towered amongst lovely sun-warmed, orange

'Loch Achlaise'
A long narrow stretch of water on the road from Sheildage to Port Henderson.

stemmed Scots firs, then we finally called it a day and turned back towards camp and a good meal. As we topped the moor road again between the two sea lochs and ran along the edge of a fir wood, we passed a car parked on the grass verge. I was intent on the road and merely gave it a passing glance which showed it was empty, but Jean, from her better vantage point in the passenger seat, suddenly said "Wow" – "my my!" and laughed. My surprised and querulous "What's wrong?" produced the unexpected reply, "U-m-m-m! the couple from that car are up the burnside in the wood having a wash and all I could see was bare skin!!" ...And the road was too narrow to let me turn back!!

Clouds were closing down over the north shore peaks as we went along our own lochside road and stopped at the plantation only long enough to pick up an armful of sticks for our fire. When we came round the last corner to the tiny burnmouth bay, our green tent was still the only one on the site, and once again as we coasted to a halt, to back and turn in beside our tent, our old friend the Cuckoo greeted us – "Coockoo!, coockoo! coockoo! coockoo!"

A meal did not take long to prepare, and then as we sat in comfort in the tent entrance, relaxing after the heat of the day and stretching lazily, we heard the faint, regular 'thump, –thump, –thump' of rowlocks and a small boat slid from the shore a few hundred yards away against the evening light. Watching their progress we did not at first realise that a net was being payed out, but the glasses showed a floating line of corks stretching out to a drum-buoy. Good luck to them anyway, and we prepared to settle down for the night.

During the night it rained off and on and the wind became gusty and rough, but the morning was dry and our usual brisk open fire soon gave us another acceptable breakfast. Washing up was never any problem, for a crystal clear streamlet off the hill came jingling down from the rocks about twenty yards from the fire, and on the high side of the road less than a hundred yards from the tent, a piped section of the same stream gave us a spout to fill a kettle or pail of drinking water. It came from a spring which ran clear even after a night of rain, merely increasing its flow and carrying with it a few suspended particles of peaty soil which soon settled to the bottom and gave beautiful fresh water for cooking tea.

Breakfast past and everything tidied again, we decided it was time we did some local sketching, so when the sun came oozing through the clouds, we set out to do a series of pen sketches of the fishing boats by the mouth of the burn, the burn itself with its most unusual little bridge carrying the road, the glen and cottages, the distant stretch to the top of the loch and other corners which seemed particularly attractive. All too soon we could see a blanket of rain blotting out the end of the loch and we dashed back to the sheltering tent just in time to keep dry. By then, however, we had a collection of subjects to finish off, and though the wind rose and it became chilly, we tucked ourselves up very cosily in the tent and painted energetically and industriously – until we felt it was high time we had a meal again. For the rest of the day until evening, it continued to be showery and overcast, and we worked on as long as we had decent light for painting inside the tent.

As we put away the dishes after the last meal of the day, the sky blew clear and the freshness of the evening encouraged us to stretch our legs before

'The Mouth of the Asdale Burn'
Looking up the loch to Poolewe and the gardens.

thinking of bed. So, although the night shadows weren't far away, we crossed the road and went up to explore the old road that seemed to serve the straggle of higher cottages on the slopes of the little valley. The ground was very wet after all the rain and the hill streams were chuckling gaily with fresh found energy, but our footwear was storm welted and waterproof and our feet remained dry and warm. That was the walk that led us up the hill to the lily loch and by the time we swung down into camp again, we were thoroughly ready for a hot chocolate drink and immediate collapse into the relaxing luxury of the sleeping bags.

The sun was with us next morning when I stretched and crawled out of the blankets and the morning promised well, with mist girdles round the high peaks and a loch surface like burnished silver. Obviously a sketching day we decided as we disposed of breakfast with little waste of time.

We knew that behind the long green island on the other side of the loch lay the sheltered naval anchorage which had seen so much activity during the hectic war years, and every now and again we heard an echoing, slow, clang – clang – clang

coming over the surface from that direction. At night too, we had noticed bright lights shining from the same spot. The faithful glasses showed that some repair or extension work seemed to be going on, and the sound was apparently coming from the beginning of a steel pile. Often late into the evening it continued, singing and sounding like the strokes of a gigantic bell even above the gusty wind. We could even hear the sound of the cook-house whistle from the canteen hut above the shore at meal times, and could see vehicles moving along the shore road to the pier. We wondered also whether the musical sounds from across the loch acted as an inspiration, or possibly a challenge, to our grey feathered friend up on the hillside, and prompted him to burst out with his – "Coockoo! – coockoo – coockoo – Tut – tut – tut – tut – tut"!!!!!

But that morning Jean wanted to sketch some corners among the local cottages, so we split company – she to her selected spots and I in the car on a quick run to Poolewe. The river was high, and with the tide full in the bridge pool was not so attractive as it is at low tide, so I went further

'Inverewe House and Gardens'
Built by Osgood MacKenzie.

round and finally settled on a broad grassy road verge to do a painting of Inverewe house as it lay gleaming white in the morning sun, against its background of magnificent trees above the colourful rocks and seaweed of the little bay.

What a splendid monument and memorial that corner remains to the grand old man whose enthusiasm and planning brought that rocky waste alive in the first place. A hundred years ago it was only a point of red sandstone projecting into the loch above a tiny bay, and a raised shingle beach. The rock carried no trees of any kind and only tiny pockets of thin heather and moor grass rooted in acid peat.

When the site of the proposed house was chosen and marked out, it was found necessary to use explosives to break up the sandstone outcrops, and surprisingly, below the hard surface it turned out that the rock was broken and porous and in places almost removable with a shovel. After the house was finished, the question of lawns and flower beds arose, so the rocks and gravel were taken out to a sufficient depth to allow for this. Soil had then to be found and carried to the site in carts and barrows, and seaweed and sand and gravelly clay from the seashore was taken up and mixed with peaty soil to form a reasonable depth of suitable earth of the best quality possible in that area. Subsequent applications of lime, manure and compost, eventually gave a nursery bed for seedling trees in hollows and pockets all round the rocks behind the house, and after many experiments and disappointing trials and replantings, the present glorious mass of trees of all types slowly took shape.

During his long life-time, Osgood MacKenzie continually carried out changes and developments; bringing in trees and flowering shrubs from various parts of the world, and gradually establishing rock pools as watergardens, flower beds, walks and paths and rustic summer houses all over the immediate surroundings, until the present internationally famous gardens were ultimately carved out of the former wilderness. The place is now one of the best known 'Scottish Gardens' and as such is visited by thousands of enthusiasts from all over the world each year. Bus parties are organised right through the year, and indeed while

'Mona and Ian's House' was on the roadside.

'Peggy's House is up above'.

I sat sketching that day, several busloads spilled out and went past the gates into the grounds. At times the drifting showers blotted out the loch and the south shore where I knew our tent lay below the hills, and I wondered how Jean was coming along with her cottage pictures. Later on, when I returned to camp for a belated mid-day meal, I found she had finished one and done part of other two in between the showers, so the time was by no means wasted.

Passing the bridge and the scattered houses on my return along the lochside road, I swung round the raised bank to the trees at the foot of the hill and discovered that our earlier seen 'road family' with the bell tent had moved and were now cosily established on the grassy raised shelf of an old road-metal quarry where they had a roaring fire going. I wondered if we would see more of them in view of their move, and as it turned out, we did! I picked up a supply of sticks again as I passed the little wood and beat it back to camp before the next shower.

During the afternoon, one of the sociable cottagers whose house had been painted by Jean, proved particularly friendly when she asked about butchers and bakers vans, and milk, etc., She was "Just after baking a scone" she said in her gloriously rich Irish/West Highland mixture brogue, and would send one of her girls over with one for our tea. And in due course, as we sat in comfort in the tent, one of the girls suddenly appeared shyly and quietly at the tent doorway through the soft drizzling rain, and we found our stock of eatables enhanced – and that was the right word – not by just 'a scone', but by a supply of scones and pancakes sufficient to give us home baking for several meals.

While she was painting that particularly colourful roadside cottage, Jean had made friends with a fluffy-haired young collie pup which was being brought up as a gift for 'Grannie' up the road. This little enthusiastic bundle of energy was kept within bounds in the cottage for safety, but alas for all good intentions – the pup got out of the house and garden the following day just as a big car came by...and the driver buried it below the short sea-grass turf down by the burnside, with profuse apologies for a tragedy he could scarcely

THE BAY,
POOLEWE.

*We did wonder if it was going to rain **every** day!!.*

have avoided.

During that first week we had rain at some time every day or night, although very often the evenings cleared and gave us a most colourful sunset. Often another small boat went out from a point a little way along the coast with one, two or three occupants bent on fishing, and the rain seemed to be completely disregarded by them. That particular evening, when the showers were chasing each other in grey banks over an otherwise oily smooth surface, at frequent intervals, a group of three took a boat out to mid loch and sat there till dusk. Looking at them with the strong binoculars, we could see that all three had handlines down and were almost constantly pulling fish aboard – but after a time we tired of watching, and as the light was going quickly and the rain had lifted, we decided on a quick walk again before bed. Up on to the road we went and turned east towards Poolewe once more, intending to do the usual mile along to the Naast valley and back. But we had not gone more than half-way when a drift of rain came whirling down off the rocks just as the road crossed a steep little stream

bed. We had no coats with us, and as there were no trees nearer than the far distance, we skidded off the road down through the dripping bracken to the stream bed and looked at the culvert where the water came through below the road. It was a flat topped opening about two feet wide by four feet high, and as the water was reasonably low and had plenty of stones, we were soon perched rather precariously in a crouching position on boulders beneath the little bridge. And just in time! It rained heavily and steadily for about ten minutes, by which time in spite of changing positions and easing our muscles every few minutes, we were a trifle cramped and sore. Added to the fact that we were, of course wearing 'the kilt' and trying to keep it out of the rising water! But of course it *couldn't* last for ever? – and didn't – eventually we unfolded ourselves and got back to the road to stretch the ache out of our backs and shoulders. A quick look at the sky was enough to set us off at a brisk walk back to the tent and bed.

Saturday morning, though temporarily dry, was dull again and windy, but after a belated breakfast had been cooked just before the fire gave up the ghost, we sat inside listening to steady rain lashing the canvas, wondering if our whole two weeks holiday was going to produce the same type of weather so typical of the West Coast at times. It was mild of course down on our sheltered ledge by the water, and we were not greatly put out at having to have an easy morning doing odd jobs and reading or finishing off some sketches. The heavy rain continued till after mid-day, so we had one of our few stove cooked meals inside the tent as everything outside was saturated.

Inverasdale (where we were) means – 'at the mouth of the Asdale burn', and on this morning the burn had risen and spread over the shingle to about four or five times its usual size, and we wondered whether any sea trout might try to go up it. We did not have any opportunity to find out, as when the rain went off the water fell as quickly as it had risen, and we had other things to do anyway. I did, however, see that some of the visitors from nearby cottages had the same idea, and one particular lad threw a 'not too dainty' dry fly over the long shallow bridge pool for what seemed to be a completely fruitless spell.

That evening we had a final walk along towards the school before turning in, and we noticed that the cars had gone from the caravan tucked into the sheltered corner by the road bridge over the burn, where four people had stayed all week. Also the 'Accommodation' and 'Bed and Breakfast' signs at the various cottages had been covered up, and that reminded us that we were on the West Coast where the next day was 'The Sabbath' and a day of rest.

Sunday morning was quiet – very quiet at first –dry, bright and warm, and over breakfast we planned to explore the coast further along the lochside out to the west and look for attractive subjects to sketch. Midmorning, therefore, found us parking the car in a small opening off the road above a stretch of bright red sand, which contrasted wonderfully with green-yellow moraine grass and the richest blue sea flecked with gloriously white breaking waves. Across the wide loch the more northerly peaks stood up in an array of blue and grey shades and shapes, and judging by the number of vehicles we saw tucked in here and there, Sunday was a popular day for

'*Firemore Sands and the little burn*'.

picnic parties at this beautiful spot.

Down on the sand we looked for shells, but footprints all over showed that others had been there before us and we only found one worth keeping – a bivalve in perfect condition. A Baltic Tellin – and what a beauty – a rich coral pink shading to cherry red, banded in white with a perfect deep pink inside. Quite perfect and firmly hinged, to add to Jean's collection. She went on looking for more while I sketched a corner where a tiny stream came curving down and over the sand to the edge of the tide, with all the colours of the rainbow visible at once.

Back over the hills to the south east, however, a tremendous area of thundery cumulus clouds was banking up, travelling fast and drawing under it a murky looking blue/purple mass that spelt trouble. On the southern edge of this mass, the heavier outflanking clouds already showed great streaks of obvious rain or hail falling at an angle, and as we were some distance from the car without coats we deemed it wise to play safe, and beat it quickly back to the shelter of the little vehicle. We were just in time for we had scarcely shut the doors when the edge of the rain hit us. And it certainly did rain for a time, spraying off the bonnet in solid sheets while we sat waiting for the worst to pass.

As soon as the wipers could deal with it properly, we turned out to the road and splashed our way back towards the camp with water flying from the wheels like a bow wave from a small boat. The worst of the rain belt seemed to have crossed the hill just in a narrow band and beyond our camping place we could see a thin patch of sun through the grey veil. In no time we were under canvas and having some lunch.

It continued to rain however, in sudden gusts and squalls and drifts, with an occasional thundery deluge for good measure, and car after car filled with would be picnic folk went splashing and hissing over the road above us as they headed home. And of course the burn rose again.

On our holiday so far we had concentrated on paintings and quick sketches, but in such an attractively wild countryside, it seemed unthinkable that the trout rods should remain in the back of the car all the time without a reasonable airing, and we were itching to

'We splashed our way back to camp past the old school'.

explore the possibilities – if we could find them! Our conversations with the villagers, therefore, had been inclined to slide round as often as possible to the matter of lochs and streams and trout fishing, and eventually one of them had mentioned a more distant group of hill lochs with quite unpronounceable Gaelic names, which were said to be worth visiting, provided we were not discouraged by the prospect of a long rough hill scramble to get there. My informant mentioned a recognisable point on a certain road for taking off into this area. Back at camp later on, I looked at the map and soon felt I had located the lochs away on the higher ground.

A good map is essential to this type of holiday exploration and it is fairly easy – with practice at least – to roughly visualise strange ground from the full valley contour and feature details now given on modern local maps. Subsequently anyone with an eye for countryside should be able to take a fairly accurate line across to a chosen objective from memory, without too much difficulty as long as the weather remains clear. In thick weather, rain or hill mist, the picture changes completely even on known ground, and the situation can become awkward and at times positively dangerous.

So in the snug warmth of the tent we made our plans – subject to weather conditions – for the following day, which was our wedding anniversary and therefore called for something different.

When we parked the car below the shelter of a high peat bank soon after breakfast next morning, the burn beside us was running full and forceful, with that very fishable, attractive looking peat water shade of swirling reddish brown flecked with white and blue sky reflections, that wakens a fisherman's high hopes. In minutes we were over the first mound out of sight of the road and moving up the little sheep track towards the big dip where we knew the loch spilled out into a stream.

As we came out of the dip of the burn on to the loch level, the wind was flicking the little waves 'slap, slap, slap' against the rocks and luckily our backs were mainly to it. The water did not look deep, but we cast round the rocks through the waves into the quieter bits over shingle and sand for about half a mile up the loch without a response, and without seeing any sign of fish of any sort. Short lashing showers kept sliding off the high ground to the lower moors, but we always had ample warning of their coming and the loch shore was a mass of particularly convenient peat bank nooks and overhangs, so that we were seldom caught out. These nooks however, were generally strung across with a network of spider's webs as thick as silk threads, mostly carrying great hairy grey-brown spiders with bulky bodies and long, crusty looking legs. Naturally enough they did not like us sitting on their webs – and Jean was not very happy either!!

Eventually on our loch circuit we came to a tributary stream which was too wide and deep to cross as we only had wellingtons on our feet, so took the obvious alternative and fished up running water for a change. Almost my first cast produced a rise, and another and another, and then a small dark trout whirled out on to the bank to be released and returned at once. So it went on over the quarter mile or so we covered. Plenty of small trout everywhere but never one that either of us could keep. By the time we stopped the total was twenty-nine without a single 'tail in the bag', but it had been a most enjoyable forenoon in spite of the rain, and we felt thoroughly ready for a good meal. The loch had produced one quick rise near the burn-mouth on the way back which might have come from a sizeable trout but was not repeated, so the water remained an unknown possibility. It looked enticing all right and under different conditions – who knows?

The afternoon was well gone when we sat down to deal most effectively with chicken, green peas, tomatoes and potato chipples. This was followed by sliced peaches and cream and topped off with a much relished cup of tea and biscuits. There is nothing like camping and outdoor exercise for giving folk a good appetite. We did not feel very energetic afterwards, I wonder why?

Some time during the evening we ran down in the car to the woods and renewed our stock of firewood, and by the time we had made our leisurely way back it was again time to think of a cuppa and bed. We had taken two library books with us and read them at odd moments when there was nothing special to do – which was not often – and actually they were only finished after we got home. The tent was made secure for the night, fresh water had been drawn from the tiny hill stream, dry wood tucked into the boot of the car for the morning, guy ropes and pegs checked, and milk heated for a cup of hot chocolate. It had been a good day and we were ready for sleep. The rain had eased off but the ground was still wet even on our very advantageous short turfy grass which drained beautifully and did not break up at all over the whole two weeks we were there. Just as we finished our drinks, we heard a car slow down on the road above us and then go on slowly. A minute or two later we heard the sound of an engine come slowly nearer and stop. We had company! A door banged and a South voice said "This is a'right!". A sound of activity and a tent peg or two being banged home, and later inspection through our peep hole in the roof of the tent revealed a moderate sized white tent and another small car had joined our outfit. It's always amusing to hear snatches of conversation when the speakers don't realise they have an audience, and it seemed the newcomers were in doubt about whether our tent was occupied or not, as we were keeping very quiet. At any rate we heard some of their remarks quite clearly enough to make us feel we would love to give them a reply!

Our neighbours wasted no time in making themselves snug for the night, and apart from one or two bangs of their car doors, they seemed to settle down almost at once. Their white tent made an excellent shadow screen when they switched on a light – but we didn't look!! We were soon tucked up in bed ourselves and the only sounds came from the shore birds and the sheep cropping the grass, and the lovely peaceful sound of the waves. An old heron suddenly said "Krank" and a couple of oyster catchers exploded in a babbling protest at something that disturbed them, then a second or two later the heron called again as she laboriously flapped past low along the water surface. High over head came the eerie, flying call of the shelduck going over the sandbank – "Kek – kek – kek – kek – kek"! A ewe and her lamb called to each other from somewhere among the higher jumble of rocks, and close at hand behind the tent the rasping, grass-cropping sound of a cattle beast came, and we waited for the inevitable sound – a guy rope twanged as it touched it, and then obviously it nosed the tent and snorted and blew loudly. I stretched out a hand from under the sleeping bag, hit the end wall canvas smartly with the flat of my hand, and was rewarded with a sudden startled snort, and grunt, a hurried scamper of hoofs to a safer distance, then a long derisive blast of exhaled breath – and silence. We couldn't help laughing before settling down to sleep at last.

HERON
STANDING LIKE AN UNTIDY
OLD GENTLEMAN.

OYSTERCATCHER

SHELDUCK
FLEW OVERHEAD.

Chapter IV

Over the breakfast fire next morning we made the acquaintance of our neighbour campers when they prospected for a water supply and enquired about milk etc. They were a couple from Paisley district as we had thought from their voices, and we learned that they had been literally washed out of their Sunday night campsite at Achnasheen, where the rain had been torrential and their shelter from the gale practically non-existent. (It reminded me of another night and another family who had been – washed out).

It happened one night when we camped near a river, on the only suitable bit of grass there was – on road level and just wide enough to take the car and the tent. The bank to the right of us sloped a little from the road to another level bit, but we had avoided that as it was obvious from the clouds that it was going to rain.

We set up camp, had something to eat and settled for the night before the rain started. Before we got to sleep we heard a car stop, and the sound of feet and voices. Oh! Oh! Right enough we heard a tent going up, feet going to and fro and then silence, and we went to sleep.

It was about two in the morning when the 'WEATHER' hit us – thunder, lightning and torrential rain – and we waited for it! Sure enough there was a sudden commotion beside us and raised voices. The car lights shone full on our tent and there was a mad scramble as everyone piled into the car and grumbling voices went on for quite some time, but eventually we got back to sleep.

We rose to a beautiful sunny morning and to the sound of – crackling sticks??... Beyond their tent our neighbours had an enormous bonfire going and everything they owned, by the look of it, was piled round it and on sticks round about. The father came over to speak when we emerged (dry and rested) and said "Mm". "It looks as though you have camped before? You were wise to put your tent on the higher bit. The water from the road ran right through ours and we got soaked. You see it's our first time" (by the look on his wife's face – it might be their last I thought!). Then when breakfast was over and I went out to shave, having noticed a handy tree branch to hang a mirror on, he again came over ruefully rubbing his chin – " and I brought an electric razor and have nowhere to plug it in"!

Our neighbours *this* time complained of feeling cold at night and when we learned about their sleeping set-up, we weren't surprised they had hot water bottles in bed with them! Their light sleeping bags were on the ground on a double thickness of tarpaulin, so in this area it would have been more surprising if they had *not* been cold. Later on we let them see our 'home from home' sleeping arrangements a full six to eight inches off the cold damp ground, and they envied us a bit.

They liked the place thoroughly, however, and intended to stay a day or two they said as they closed the tent and left in their car after breakfast. We didn't see them again until evening, after we had returned from a piece of exploration we had had in mind all the previous week. The road past our camp went west out to the headland and the open sea for several miles as indicated on our map, and we wanted to sample it's attractions, so after a leisurely morning doing a bit of washing etc., we took the car over the nearby skyline and along past our furthest point at the red sands – (which we found out was called Firemore Sands). The run gave us another endless series of paintable little views and corners. The sun was out and was very warm and bright, and without the usual bothersome breeze we had the car windows open as we glided along. Blue bays with lovely white topped breakers, brilliant sand and dark red cliffs, merely made a background to white cottages tucked into sheltered corners; boats old and new, buildings of old rich stonework and rippling, sparkling streams among grassy mounds. All this made up for the rainy conditions and made us forget them. It was glorious.

Far out past the last houses the road deteriorated into a rough surface full of atrocious potholes, but the tracks of earlier cars still went on and so, carefully, did we. Rounding a gradual curve we came in sight of the end of the road and a rough footpath going over the mounds ahead towards the sea.

Wl over to Mellon Charles from the old Fort - Loch Ewe.

These mounds were crowned with strange looking flattish pillbox sort of shapes with long slits in the sides, while alongside the track we were on we could see numerous base foundations in concrete which had very obviously supported army huts or buildings of some sort. Between and around these ran a network of narrow white stony paths and we went up to investigate them.

That old former coastal defence post simply overflowed with a ghostly atmosphere and the echoes of voices, I felt, and it was with a somewhat unconscious military swagger that I strode around with the kilt swinging, from one vantage point to another! The old gun-sites were tremendous erections of steel and concrete, though the salt sea air of twenty odd years had promoted a growth of rusty flakes over the exposed metal beams.

The ammunition niches were still there behind the gun mountings, concrete steps were sound and solid, and a whole collection of smaller buildings still remained at various points giving little indication of their original purpose. We followed a rough path over the last grassy mound and circled round a narrow gully running in from the sea, but when I approached the edge carefully on bent knees and knuckles, I discovered I was perched on a flat projecting shelf of rock which overhung the boiling purple-blue water of a gully about fifty feet below. My hasty glance showed the water swirling madly back into a high narrow cave as the swell came in from the open sea, with a roar and a "woof" – and then I was scrambling back to my feet again and – "getting to blazes" out of there in a hurry. It was no place to linger on.

Back to safer ground again, we admired the small patches of pinkish stonecrop in nooks in the rocks and a few purple spotted wild orchids in damp patches, and regretted the restriction that flying time and healthy appetite put on more extensive exploration of the great stretch of rough ground which still lay out to the west of the site. A piece of chocolate and a biscuit staved off the worst of the hunger pangs for the moment, and then we followed still another beautifully laid concrete slab path winding up to what appeared to be a flagstaff site for the camp – a flat area of turf surrounded by a low, circular boundary wall with

several paths leading up to it. But this place too had a distinctly eerie feel even in that bright sunshine and we soon felt we had been there long enough. On a rough dark night, or a dull day of sea fog with the seawind moaning in the rock gullies, it would be no place for the imaginative visitor.

There were no small pieces of metal or wire lying around anywhere and I suspected that our scrap merchant in the brown tent, or even souvenir hunters, had already gleaned all the movable pieces. This view was confirmed by our next contact.with the blue lorry the following day, but for the moment we turned back towards camp and a meal. The late afternoon was still gloriously warm on our side of the sea inlet, but looking out and over to the north coastline, we could see white teeth gleaming round all the rocky points, and the roar of the Atlantic swell beating against the headlands with great bursts of spray, gave the explanation of the sound we had heard from our camp at intervals earlier in the week.

When we slid down again from the road to our site, the white tent was still closed and silent and we busied ourselves smartly with the preparation

SEA THRIFT

and disposal of our meal. That past and the washing up done, we took the chance to slip down to Poolewe again in the car to renew our petrol supply and get one or two items at the store. The brown tent was still in its sheltered corner as we passed, but the lorry was off out somewhere. A sudden showery drift came out of a cloud at the back of the hill when we ran up into the scrubby

The view from our tent over the burn mouth.

tree sheltered section of the road on the way back, but we stopped long enough to stock up on firewood sufficient to last for the rest of our stay, before going on to our homely corner by the distant cottages.

The light had that indescribable soft pearly grey composition that indicates low drifting, misty clouds with sunshine behind it, and the surface of the loch had gone oily smooth and silvery. We looked at the scene full of atmosphere with a distant indication of rain over what remained visible of the far peaks, and I felt impelled once more to attempt to capture that elusive light on paper, with the rich colourful stretch of seaweed covered shore by the burn mouth giving the whole thing depth. So I sat at the door of the tent and painted for the next hour while the effect lasted, then a billy of tea became the most immediate need and the kettle was soon swinging from the wire hook over a crackling fire. A billy of tea is most welcome when we're in camp, and though the kettle provides four big mugs there is usually nothing left but tea leaves – but fresh spring water and a seasoned kettle do make glorious tea.

By the time we finished, the sky had cleared and there was excellent promise of another clear evening, so, when our camping neighbours came back and the ladies got into a chin-wagging discussion of the day's events, I slung the binoculars over my shoulder and went off up the hill beyond the road and behind the houses. By the garden wall of the last house in the group, a narrow track went up to a wicket gate that opened on to the slope of the hill, and I followed the old "Brae" road a few yards above until it met the boundary wall which climbed steeply to the rugged skyline some hundreds of feet up. There I turned uphill and scrambled steadily with frequent rests, up through the rocks and trickling water beds, over slippery sheep cropped grass patches and banks of slimy clay and loose stones, round rocky outcrops and through occasional bracken patches, till I came to another tiny gate where the slope levelled temporarily. At that stage there were 'bellows to mend' and I was glad to lean on the old wall and unsling the glasses for a long look round. The houses of the village straggled off up the coast road into the distance, and away over and beyond them, behind the headland on the other side of the water, the knobbly shapes of the coastline hills went mistily into the haze as they disappeared north.

Down practically at my feet, as it seemed when I adjusted the glasses, I could see one of the holiday makers switching a long dry fly line over the bridge pool. Even at that distance I could see the spray flying each time he cast and see the fly land on the water surface, so clear was the hill air. So far as I saw he caught nothing. Far over the top of the glen beyond the cottages, the evening glow in the west was brilliantly reflected on the surface of the loch we had fished without success, and near the far shore the high moor bank left a duplicating shadow over a big area. I cast a casual glance over it, looked again, stared, and swung the glasses round. Glory – I *was* seeing right. Even so far away, the glasses gave an excellent definition of countless trout rising along that shore. Where they broke the surface, the rippled water at once picked up the peach sky reflection, and there was no doubt at all, that loch did contain trout of a decent size and seemingly plenty of them. We were apparently unlucky with our choice of day and time when we paid our earlier visit. But there was another sheet of water I wanted to see again and I went scrambling on, down through the rocks, across a tiny peat bog and up the far slope to a bare rocky outcrop towering against the sky. As I went forward over the grey weathered slabs, the reedy loch we had visited about a week ago came into sight, and I moved on to a seat where I could see most of it. Again the setting was the same as the one I had scanned from further down the hill. Areas of dark shadow were covered with little peach circles, and using the glasses I could see splashing rises of numerous small trout. So there were trout in this loch too, and the movement we had seen on our first evening visit was probably caused by fish after all.

This smaller lochan wandered about in the dip in long reedy arms and inlets and away to the far left corner there was a small island which sported – what? a post or a small tree stump or what? again the glasses gave the answer. It was our friend the heron standing knee-deep in what looked like bog myrtle on the edge of the island,

and from his tense looking attitude he was obviously looking at me. He didn't move as I watched him, but when I scanned the distant moors for some time and picked out two other very distant patches of water, I switched back to the loch and found out the sly old 'fisherman' had moved about ten feet or so to the reed bed at the end of the island and was still watching me.

There was a draught of thin night wind on the tops by that time, so I turned back off the rocks and retraced my steps. Crossing the second ridge next to the camp, I came again in sight of some of the mid-distant cottages, and pausing to look at them again, I saw beside one of them something I could not quite make out at the foot of a tall pole where the house track went in from the road. When I put the glasses on the object I almost jumped, and could scarcely help chuckling softly to myself. I was looking straight at one of the crofters who was looking at me, through *his* binoculars! For no reason at all, I felt rather guilty, as though I had been caught peeping, and I hastily lowered my glasses and turned down towards camp and supper.

That drop off the skyline down the dips and zig-zag sheep tracks to the road level, was a whirlwind descent that jarred the heels and thigh muscles which luckily were in good trim after our activity of the past ten days, and it was at a controlled and careful half run that made the kilt fly. In no time I was back by the camp fire. Supper and bed were the next items on the programme, and while Jean got the beds down, I coaxed the little fire into life and boiled the kettle. Our friends were also preparing supper prior to turning in early after their long day exploring the countryside, and in the middle of these preparations there came a sudden splash from the edge of the full tide a few yards below the tents. That was a sea-trout amongst the seaweed tangles and a good one too judging by the splash.

The sound of that fish reminded us that our holiday was drawing quickly to a close and we still had not done much fishing, so over our hot drinks we made plans for the remaining days. At the same time bemoaning the sad fact that, as always in such circumstances, we just did not have enough time to do half of the things we wanted to do.

The bay at Firemore with Stirkhill Point

Breakfast next morning was a brisk meal with no dallying, and we were off as soon as possible in brilliant sunshine, on a quick run along to Firemore Sands to try to do another picture. We settled eventually in a spot rather open to the chilly wind, but the view was brilliant with rich colour and the discomfort did not count for very much. While we sat painting, the pale blue scrap lorry came over the rise of the road and turned down on to the headland in front of us, obviously familiar with the ground and stopping frequently to pick up some small thing here and there.

The man gave us a long look as he went past, no doubt recognising the car parked nearby, which also received a curious stare as he came back to the road and went on into the distance towards the old camp.

The call of the inner man for something warm finally made me pack up my paint box and give Jean a whistle, and before very long she came over to join me in the snug shelter of the car which, sitting full in the sun was like a small hot-house. Then it was a case of back to the tent again for a good warm meal. Our friends in the white tent were having a quiet day for a change, and we found 'Nan' stretched out full length in the sun on a travelling rug, happily reading and sun-bathing. Her husband was down at the end of the nearby stone jetty trying his luck with a small spinning rod and float tackle, a pastime which to us who were used to brisk fly fishing on streams, seemed to demand the last word in patience.

The road along which we went to do our long bit of fishing.

Chapter V

After our meal we sat at the end of the tent in the shade and shelter from the wind, painting for an hour or two, then following the plan we made, we had a quick cup of tea and just before five o'clock left camp in the car again with the fishing things and a bit of food.

Now it's a well known fact that fishermen as a general rule do not speak too freely of fishing spots discovered and visited, and since the exact location of our visit has no bearing on this account, I'll merely say that in due course we ran down a small slope to a tiny stream in an open hill glen which matched the mental picture I retained from the map. Very soon the car was tucked off the road and we were over the roadside ditch on to ground which proved to be turfy and firm and surprisingly dry. The first ten minutes or so took us up a branch burn into a fold of the hills out of sight of the road, and we continued towards a selected point on the distant skyline. These slopes above the small glen were natural drainage areas, and the ground was full of little runnels winding down from mossy patches among the peat which went round the grey rocky outcrops on all sides. Yellowish wiry patches of moor grass were everywhere, with tiny beds of bracken down by the dancing, winding stream, and sheep tracks following the contours of each mound through countless patches of short bristly heather.

Gradually we climbed on to bare rocky ground from which we could see over into a big hollow to our left, and eventually a small narrow loch rose into view – the first of the ground checks to our anticipated goal. Before long a second small loch appeared a little higher up, and away ahead over a long stretch of waving and dipping yellow brown moorland, we caught a glimpse of another larger sheet of water lying below a backing of higher hills. That was apparently our objective, but even in the full knowledge that distances in hill country can be extremely deceptive, we thought it still looked a long way off. At that point our line of advance dropped off the rocky ground into a long dip sloping towards the loch, and we were soon down on a mixed carpet of brown and green grass and moss which looked treacherous, – and proved to be a regular, spongy, moisture-oozing mass!

Crossing it was soon obviously impossible even with our heavy-welted waterproof shoes, and we had to angle away up to the right towards the top of the dip in the hope of finding drier ground we could safely use. It proved a rather forlorn hope as the saddle between the two rocky areas held a peat moss pocket from which water drained out in opposite directions towards the parallel glens on either side. It took us some time and many tentative trials, to pick our way like leaping deer across the drier tufts of heathery rushy ground to the edge of the firmer moor beyond, but eventually we were over at the expense of only one wet foot, (and a terrified wife who hates swampy ground)!

We were then considerably off our direct course towards where we had seen the distant loch, and we started to contour back along the hillside to get back to our line. As our view of the loch widened, we saw a figure seated on the bank at the near end of the water – fairly obviously a fisherman though there was no sign of a rod. Now we did not know and certainly had not enquired whether these lochs were restricted as to fishing, except possibly for local enthusiasts, so we turned as naturally as possible off the skyline and continued along the slope without looking towards the loch. Curving round the hill over heathery tussocks, rocks and small peaty ditches, we soon had the loch back in view, and as we trudged steadily forward to the far edge of the moor where the ground fell away to the loch basin, we found ourselves looking down a long swinging slope to a narrow inlet bay which tapered out to a little stony beach. From this, two figures were moving off slowly along the edge of the loch, the leading one male, casting a fly-line as he went, while his female companion followed a dozen or so paces behind.

As we topped the slope they looked up and back at us for a long minute, then as we kept on steadily towards the water they moved on steadily over the lochside boulders, casting and glancing back at us. About twenty yards from the water we sat on a rock to let them clear the area before we started to fish and to see if there was any sign of fish rising anywhere. I was watching the two quickly receding figures when Jean said "There's a rod lying amongst the rocks just in front of us". So there was – a substantial looking one – and we assumed it must belong to the lady of the pair we could still see round the curve of the loch shore, though we wondered why she should have left it there so trustingly. Perhaps that was the reason why they kept looking back at us so often. As I looked at the rod and the water behind it, a movement against the skyline attracted my attention, and the fisherman we had seen earlier lower down the loch, came down to a small rugged point across the bay from our rocky seat. Shading his eyes from the sun glare with his hand, he peered up the loch into the distance and then, looking round the nearer landscape, spotted us down below and had another long look before moving slowly down to the water's edge. Not knowing who he might be, but keeping Scotland's social 'niceties' in mind, I called across to him, asking if he was looking for two other fishers. The wind on his side of the bay must have drowned my question, however, because he did not reply until he had come round to our side of the inlet, and I repeated my question as he approached us. He was not looking for anyone, it seemed, just wondering whether my part of the water was any more productive than the bit he had tried, as this was his first time on this loch. I confessed similar ignorance of the water, merely remarking that in such water trout were often to be found feeding on the windward shore where the choppy waves stirred up food.

The inlet in front of us was showing a smooth surface of shallow looking unruffled water, but beyond the point across that stretch, a line of rough, breeze-swept water cut over at a long angle to our shore about a hundred yards or more to the right. Seemingly our friend accepted the hint, because he passed a conventional remark or two before turning off along the edge towards the rougher water. After watching him for a few minutes, Jean and I put our rods together. Then she said – "There's a fish splashing in the rough water just outside that rock across at the point. It rose while you were talking and it came up again just now".

Round I went to the broken water where the wind proved to be suddenly remarkably cold, but though I cast repeatedly over the spot where the trout had shown I had no response. The water was stony and not too deep near the edge but the breeze made a big difference, and the main difficulty lay in getting the fly out into a decent fishing position. The water on the other side of the point went into another long inlet, and we went along to the more sheltered end below the high moor mounds where the surface was less ruffled and casting much easier. We fished that shore right back to the point but no trout were rising anywhere, and from the only two rises I had, one trout was landed and the other lost almost at the edge.

The fish I kept was a curious looking one, silvery sided and white bellied with a few small dark spots and a dark olive-green back and small head. I remembered catching one of the same type years before in another hill loch on the north coast and it seemed that this big loch bred the same sort of fish. They were certainly strong fighters and very active. While I was having a break and Jean was fishing, I became conscious that some sort of musical sound was being carried in faint echoes across the water. I listened carefully with one ear turned out of the breeze, and it seemed that the notes came from the rock face of the hill across the loch. Then came a small spell of clearer definition and I realised I was listening again to the clanging, bell-like notes of the pile driver at the naval pier goodness knows how many miles away.

The sun was down by this time and the wind seemed to be still rising away up on the tops, so with the memory of our long tramp back to the car keenly in mind, we packed up the rods and started back. No one else was in sight though we had caught glimpses now and again of two figures moving slowly on the far side of the water which I thought must be the pair we had seen when we arrived. As we left the loch a raven flew high overhead with heavy wing beats, heading north into the afterglow towards some distant cliff ledge, and we heard his harsh "Croak" – "Croak" long after we had lost sight of him. The light was still strong and clear, but we did not relish the thought of having to pick our way through boggy ground again on the way back, so we struck uphill from the loch end on to firm heathery turf. When

RAVEM.

I had studied the map earlier, I had noted that a path was indicated through this district, and since it seemed to pass roughly parallel to the loch on the slope of the moor, we went uphill looking for it as an easier means of return. Quite high up above the loch we found it – not a beaten track by any means, but quite recognisably a path and not a sheep track.

How much more easily we could move along on that path and how sensibly and well it avoided the soft patches and spring heads. It must have been used as a pony bridle path at one time as there were no unduly steep bits anywhere, and at numerous places where wet peat could not be avoided, stones had been sunk to make a rough causeway. The tops of these boulders were fairly smooth worn indicating long use, and I wondered whether it was, in fact, one of the droving tracks used in earlier days for driving cattle to main marketing centres. It was very welcome anyway.

The track followed a more direct route on higher ground than we had come on the way up, which explained why we had not seen it at any point, but when we had crossed over the first small hill and dropped down on the far side I realised we were coming back to the wet saddle where we had the spot of bother earlier. It had been very noticeable all the way over from the loch that stones appeared everywhere on the direct line of the path in a faintly traceable light grey line which, now that we knew exactly what to look for, could be seen crossing the rising ground some distance ahead in zig-zag snatches.

We dropped down through a thin film of trickling water on the track to the edge of the marshy bit and discovered that, on our side, a couple of stones lay partly hidden among the moss and took us within easy jumping distance of another on the far side. So much for our wasted time on the way up – we had missed the stepping stones by about a couple of yards! At that point the path diverged somewhat to the left round the slope above the marsh, then went straight up over a series of long rough rocky patches where again the actual track showed lighter, and finally cut down a stretch of turfy grass like a miniature gully between the rocks to angle round the next mound and disappear among more rocks. So it went on, as did we, happily and easily and by then glowing with fresh air and healthy exercise. The cold wind of the loch side was forgotten and we were much more sheltered by then, having come down a considerable way. The cottage on the braeside came into sight again and we could see the car down below.

It was almost eleven o'clock when we put the rods back in the car and pulled out on to the narrow road for the run home to camp. A hot drink of creamy chocolate and some biscuits made a welcome finish to a grand outing, and though we had very little to show for it, we were thoroughly pleased with our exploratory jaunt. The moon was showing faintly through fast travelling clouds above Loch Ewe as we closed the tent and stretched out in the sleeping bags. A light or two across the water at the worker's camp showed that someone was still on the move, and a single light in an upper floor of the big old red sandstone house on the far side of the burn mouth suggested someone might be reading, or possibly just getting dressed, as the tide was up, and that was when the small boat usually crept out from the shore. A few minutes later a startled curlew suddenly rose calling quickly as it circled, and from the sound, seemed to go back up the burn towards the moor, and I wondered aloud if the sea-trout net was again working the flood tide – but I got no response, Jean was fast asleep and I followed her example.

Beinn Airidhchaar (pronounced Ben Arichar) and the sheep 'fank'
our constantly changing view.

Chapter VI

The following morning was again dry and the smell of breakfast was soon filling the tent with the usual appetising aroma of bacon, eggs, sausages and tomato, and we felt really hungry after the exercise of the previous evening but did not waste too much time with it, this being the last day of our holiday plus the fact that we were faced with an unexpected problem. On the way home the night before I had noted that the dynamo was not charging, and examination showed a broken fan-belt, luckily still lying on the engine mounting, so a replacement had to be found before our long journey home next day. I mentioned the mishap to our friends in the other tent and 'Bob', who was a motor engineer by trade, offered to help rig something temporarily if we failed to get a new one in the district. It was a nice offer, but as it turned out we did not need to take advantage of it. His wife, incidentally, when she appeared out of the tent, showed a face almost unbelievably disfigured with swellings from a very bad dose of

CURLEW.
WITH THE HAUNTING CALL
" COOR-LI "

sunburn – the result of her rather unwise sun-bathing the previous day. She could scarcely see out of either eye so badly puffed up were they, and her cheeks and lips were also badly swollen. Jean could only offer some Savlon which helped a little, but their programme consisted of an attempt to contact someone who could prescribe something to help and they left early with that intention. It turned out later that they failed to contact either a doctor or nurse and only with difficulty obtained a cooling lotion from a shop in Gairloch. At any rate there was not much they could do that day but keep out of the sun.

The nearest repair garage was beyond Poolewe, and there we went slowly and carefully keeping our fingers crossed, with that infernal cuckoo hurling derision at us as we left camp! The garage proprietor was a bearded young highlander of the usual pleasant, helpful type, though he was not too hopeful of being able to help us. He asked if I still had the old belt and went off with it to his store. One after another belt was produced, glanced at then discarded. "Too big – too small – that's no use – no, I'm sorry, I'm afraid I haven't got your size at all now. There are so many cars on the road at this time of year, and I don't get much chance to renew my stock of the popular sizes". All this and many indecipherable grunts and exclamations while he still continued to search and examine, then ... "Look now, let me see your one again – this might do. The engine mounting could be adjusted a bit". And it was, and with a little juggling and the use of a thin steel crowbar, the new belt was in place.

As he finished the adjusting of the mountings, a second figure which I casually took to be his assistant, came over to look on, and I remarked. "He managed it". I wondered vaguely why he merely grinned and said nothing, and was still puzzled a second or two later when I picked up the crowbar as the bonnet closed, offered it to him, and was again rewarded with a grin and a slight shake of the head. The bearded highlander immediately took the crowbar and turned back into the garage store, where I followed him to pay my debt and express my gratitude for his trouble. He said nothing about the crowbar and it was only after I had returned to the car that Jean chuckled and explained. As we pulled away from the garage, she said – "Didn't you notice, that was the scrap hawker you tried to give the crowbar to?" No wonder he just grinned and said nothing! The blue scrap lorry had apparently pulled in to the pumps while we were busy with the belt, but I hadn't noticed it, nor recognised the young sunburnt fellow out of it.

We turned uphill by the river and went on laughing at this finish to the belt episode; then on the steep brae beyond we came suddenly up to an enormous curly horned black faced ram with its horns stuck in the roadside fence wires. These sheep are very heavy animals and as strong as horses, and though I got out of the car and went back to it, I did so rather carefully, and as soon as I gripped his horns I knew I could not push him against his will. However, though I could not budge *him*, I could manoeuvre the fence wire a bit and he was soon free to cross the road to the hill, trotting slowly in a dignified manner and shaking his head as he went.

Now there was another loch I wanted very much to visit, and since this was my last chance, we pushed on over the moor road and continued till we reached a point near the chosen water where an old branching track offered a parking place for the car. Jean elected to remain in the car and finish a picture on which she had been working, so off I went on my own across the peat banks. Glancing round as a vehicle went past, I saw the blue lorry once more and the driver waved a friendly greeting from the cab. We did not see them again and their campsite was empty when we passed it later.

The ground I was on was wet and full of peat holes, so I had to keep circling round and jumping to drier tufts, as I had quite unthinkingly gone away from the car wearing the thick soled gym shoes I sometimes use when I'm driving from camp. It turned out to be a lucky choice later, however, as the light footwear allowed me to skip over the ground quite quickly and I was on the near shore of the loch before long. It was stony and wet in places where the water trickled in from the peat, but the bottom of the loch itself seemed to be level and as far as I could see there was no weed. Here and there a rocky outcrop stuck above the water but there was no sign of trout rising near me, possibly because the water seemed fairly shallow and was clear of the effect of the breeze which came over the moor at my back.

I tried a few casts as I moved towards the near end of the loch into the edge of the breeze, but the water in the bay was, if anything, even shallower

THE HILL LOCH.

crouched forward amongst the rocks to a squatting seat on a smooth flat slab. The water was beautifully clear, and I could see the yellowish rock go sloping out below the surface for a few yards before it stopped and showed a satisfactory dark area which suggested a shelf and a drop to deeper water.

As usual I was casting a home-made fly, and the one I had on then was a Rhode Island hackle spider with a red wool body silvered ribbed, which sank a little as I worked it along. A fairly long cast out beyond the point was brought in for a yard or so and then the cast seemed to lift momentarily, just a trifle out of the expected rhythm. A quick strike brought no resistance, however, and I wondered if I had perhaps touched a rock, so I recovered the line and cast again about a yard into the wind from the previous spot, since loch trout are very often notorious cruisers. Again as the fly approached the rock there came that slight check, but this time on the edge of the strongest ripple, and I caught a golden glint below the water. Still no contact however, and no further offer. I moved a few feet, still crouching, and cast into the breeze

and I had no response. Amongst the broken rocks an outlet stream went out but was comparatively easily crossed, and I hurried round the edge into a brisker breeze which raised a nice ripple. A bay with a firm small gravel shore and nicely shelving water gave no encouragement at all, then as I went round towards where a flat rocky point set out into the water, I saw the splash of a moving trout well out in the stronger breeze area. There were trout there, at any rate. The breeze was coming in nicely from a 'two o'clock' angle as I line about ten or fifteen feet from the rocky point. Almost at once the check came again with another quick under water flash and this time my strike was solid. The trout remained deep and tried to run into rocky ledges but I jockeyed him back into the bay, and finally on to a tiny watery shelf on the rock where I secured him. He was a nice three quarter pound fish, firm and beautifully marked and a very acceptable contribution to the menu.

I moved a little further round the tiny bay and cast repeatedly without encouragement then, remembering the first gleam seen at the point as fishermen will do, I slipped back to my first flat rock and cast again. A trout rose with a flat sort of swirl well out beyond my fly, and though I lengthened line at once and cast near him he ignored me, so again I shortened line and cast just clear of the visible rock edge. The fly sank pretty well, and as the pluck I felt was quite light, I was sure I had touched the edge of the shelf, but I cast quickly out again on the off-chance, and the repeated touch and quick response sent another trout diving for the shadows. He was landed in the same way as the earlier one as I had left the landing net in the back of the car, but he was a shade smaller than the first fish.

From that result it seemed as though the rocky points were productive, so I moved along to the next one round the bay and tried again. The water there looked deeper and produced no result, so again I went on, casting casually as I went. Round the next bend a fairly big flattish stone stood out of the water about 20 feet from the shore, and a series of smaller stone tops lay between, tempting a tight rope act. So far as I could see the water was just about six inches deep over small shingle, so I could not get very wet if I went in – unless I *fell* in, of course – and with my light rubber soled shoes to keep a grip on the dry rock tops, I just made it in a series of rather hesitant steps and stretches. Luckily there were no loose stones in the lot.

The water beyond the last rock was darker and deeper looking and nicely rippled, but ten minutes of persistent casting here and there might as well have been done in a bath tub for all the result it produced – and I was faced with the return to the bank. Somehow it did not look so straightforward from out there but I reached it with nothing worse that a toe splash on the last section. I was beginning to feel peckish by then so hurried back along the shingle, tried one point quickly and a bay probably too quickly, then came back to the productive point of rock once more and crouched down. One touch came far out but was not repeated and I turned back to the heather bank and on to the crisp shingle of the bay towards the burn. Casting as I went I had not gone far when, recovering a cast, I saw a rise close in off the point I had just left. Back I went and waited just clear of the rocks, and in a few seconds it rose again coming across the bay. The first quick cast seemed to land too near, but I moved it jerkily and almost at once came a heavy swirling rise and an immediate solid weight at the strike. This one knew a thing or two, and headed out as hard as he could, then jumped. It looked a beauty, but it was soundly hooked and I soon brought it back onto the shingle and ran it up the beach.

It was a beautiful pound plus fish, thick and deep with a lovely small head and big red spots below an olive-green back. Then I thought of Jean

in the car and the fact that my stomach said it was dinner-time, and packed up well satisfied with my short spell on the water. We were late for lunch by the time we slid back into camp but immediately I

cleaned and boiled the big trout. He was as red as a salmon and had to be cut in two to fit into the pan. We let him cool there in the juice, and were just preparing to sit down to a most appetising looking meal of half the fish when our camping neighbours came back. When we presented them with the second half of the fish, gloriously aromatic in its salmon-pink state, they lost no time

Looking up the burn to the road.

in disappearing into their tent to sample it. I don't remember what else we had to that meal but there certainly was nothing left of the trout.

When we had finished, we noticed a big duck-like bird with a long thin neck swimming a good way out from the shore and diving frequently. The glasses showed him to be a black-throated diver very busily catching himself numerous fish which he held across his bill till they stopped wriggling, then swallowed quickly, afterwards washing his bill energetically before going after another one. He slid off further along the shore when a rival fisherman appeared from the tent next door bound for the jetty again with his small rod, no doubt inspired to some extent by the trout.

We painted again while the sun lasted, but the end of loch soon disappeared under a grey drift and we had to dodge inside again. Our friends from the white tent came over to look at our pictures before we parted next day, and we yarned for some time about camping and camping spots, outfits and comfort in camp generally, before they went off to make tea and we cooked the remaining two trout. We had just finished this when the rain came on

again and continued well through the evening. We knew we had a long run again the next day over to the Black Isle, so we did a little packing up and then sat reading contentedly and snugly until after nine o'clock when the rain lifted and the sky cleared.

Jean had a small painting of the cottage up the road to give to our kindly friend there who had supplied us with the pancakes and scones, so we made up our beds, left things ship-shape, and taking our plastic macs just in case, went up to the cottage to hand over the small souvenir prior to a last short walk and bed. The lady was delighted, and when she discovered we were off for a short walk she insisted that we should go in for a cup of tea when we came back. "Och it won't be too late" she assured us, "we don't bed very early here and I'll be making a cup anyway".

There was a branch road on the little glenside that we had not yet explored and we headed that way, but had not gone far when we saw another shower come across the hill and drift quickly towards us. At a bend in the narrow road, an old track went through a field to a couple of ruined

WILD ORCHIS

COTTON GRASS OR BOG COTTON

WHOLE FIELDS OF IT

IN MOIST GROUND

cottages with parts of collapsed roofs still standing, and we dived down there for some shelter. A sheet of rusty corrugated iron still hung in place in one of them leaving a small area of shelter underneath, and there we crouched while a heavy shower skidded off the metal and the stormy looking cloud-tossed sky gradually cleared to bring some thin light back into the landscape. When the hill had cleared and the rain dropped to a thin drizzle, we buttoned up our macs and started smartly back, for it was by then nearly eleven o'clock and we felt rather ashamed to go to any door at that time of night. On the stretch of partly marshy moor ground by the roadside, we saw a whole field of bog cotton and noticed numerous wax-white spikes of what seemed to be fragrant White Orchid, and we spared a quick inspection for possible later identification from our wild flower book before we went splashing along the pool strewn road in our (thankfully worn) wellingtons.

We need not have worried about 'Mona' as she turned out to be – she was waiting for us with a small table covered in sandwiches and home bakes and a very welcome cup of tea. Her eldest daughter had waited up too, dressed in a smart neat frock for 'the company'. They talked of their district, the people, their interests and social activities, weddings, functions and so on, and then brought out photographs for us to see in response to some remark of Jean's and the time flew towards midnight before we knew it. Then they wanted to know whether we had been there before, where we had been during our two weeks stay, what we had done and wanted to see our other paintings so Jean nipped back to the tent for them, while I answered the question about whether we had fished at all? That started us on where we had been with the rod, and when I mentioned our long walk to the big loch in the hill, Mona suddenly showed a particular interest.

"Did you go *there*? – Did you not think it was a long way? – *When* were you there?" I told her when we had done the walk and when we got back, and her next query was a trifle hesitant. – "Did you see anybody at all then?" I wondered for a split second what lay behind the question but replied that we did see two other people fishing. Again the

slight hesitation as she asked.– "Were they together, or alone – was one of them a young fellow?" By this time her husband was grinning. I said "Yes, one of them seemed to be a young man and the other could have been a girl." Then she said – "Oh! that would be ...." and mentioned a name. We told her about the two who had moved off quickly round the loch, and of the rod lying among the rocks, and the older fisherman, and that we had only brought back one trout because it was possibly too cold a night. And she smiled roguishly and said "I have a dozen trout in the fridge now that were caught that night" and laughed. Then she told us how it was done!

"I got them next morning from the couple you saw!". It was rather an anticlimax to our fishing foray but explained a lot and was, in any event no concern of ours.

After twelve thirty we managed to tear ourselves away from the comfortable chairs and the fireside, donned our wellingtons and macs again and made our way quietly back to the tent and bed. It was dry overhead and the moon showed in flashes through high, wind driven clouds, and

Poolewe on our way home.

we hoped it would remain fair so that we could pack up dry and safely in the morning. The morning was dry when we rose, and though heavy cloud trailed off the top of the hills to the east, the gaps showed an acceptable glow somewhere beyond which gave promise of sunshine later on the eastern side – and so it turned out. The tent was sponged over to get rid of the dew, and as soon as breakfast was over we started packing.

The other couple had a quick breakfast, bundled up their tent hastily and threw the rest of their things in the back of the car, and after shaking hands for the last time, set off. They were a friendly couple though we never learned their surname, and they were bound for Lochinver away to the north that night. We were the lucky ones that time, our tent was packed dry and everything stowed away before it clouded over and the wind rose as we said hasty farewells to our hostess of the night before. It was raining before we had left the lochside road, and though it improved as we ran east, the strong wind which was luckily on our backs, increased as we crossed the high ground beyond Loch Maree, and we wondered, looking back at the cloud-capped peaks further north, how our late neighbours were faring?

Our main concern was whether we would find our Black Isle site vacant but in this we were lucky again and had our cosy spot to ourselves. And once more it needed to be sheltered, because the wind kept high and did not fall with the sun as it so often does. Our protecting screen of scrubby trees once more proved a blessing, and though we had a slight shower just before we rose on Saturday morning, the continuing breeze dried the canvas and the ropes very quickly and we had no trouble. We were in no particular hurry that morning as we had no camping ground to look for and we spent more time folding and packing things neatly for the last time. Our only concern was to reach the shops in Muir of Ord before they shut at mid-day, and this we managed before turning south on the main road to Inverness and the Moray Firth coast.

Again, as we had done at the end of previous trips, we left the main road at Elgin and branched off on to the Rothes/Dufftown route, to go home

LOCH CHROISG, ACHNASHEEN.
(ON THE WAY HOME.)

A very quick sketch

by the Cabrach and Donside, and still the following wind kept us company and bowled us easily along. Going up the slope of the moor to the little pass above Glen Fiddich, I noticed a sporty looking car come romping up behind, and as we topped the rise and I glanced in the mirror I noticed that something appeared to be hanging down beneath the car like a buckled exhaust pipe. As we slid down the hill I signalled him to stop and he pulled up in front of me, but as I sprang out and went towards him, the driver emerged with his hands in his duffle-coat pockets and a deerstalker capping a half-quizzical grin. I suppose he anticipated my remark especially as I bent down to try to see under his car, for when I said. "Have you a broken exhaust pipe hanging down?" he laughed and said – "No, its a patent anti-splash device I fixed, but it seems to be giving a great number of people a great deal of amusement!". Rather "sarcy" I thought, but maybe justified if he had been stopped several times by the same type of enquiry.

A little further on we felt it was time we had our last cup of 'camp-style' tea, and pulled off the road into a convenient road-metal hole in perfect shelter where the little stove gave us no trouble. And so without hurry and without further incident of any sort, we came easily back on well-kent roads to the 'Beleaguered City by the sea', as the South Newspapers had described Aberdeen a few weeks before!

The garden looked a mess of weeds as usual on return from holiday, and it seemed as though our cats had been having a great time. Was it fancy, as we carried the camping things into the house, or did that darned Starling on the chimney top try to say "Cuckoo"? We blew him a raspberry which made him cock his head sideways, and went inside. We were home – but we vowed to go back to our little 'home' in the West next year – "God willing" as our friends over there said, as we left.

In the next book – we go further afield ....

From Melvaig across 'The Minch' to Skye

Original watercolours and prints by R.H. Eadie can be purchased from the publisher, Mrs J.M. Eadie.